Soul of Venice

A GUIDE TO 30 EXCEPTIONAL EXPERIENCES

WRITTEN BY SERVANE GIOL AND THOMAS JONGLEZ
PHOTOS BY FRANCESCA LANARO
ILLUSTRATED BY CLARA MARI

JONGLEZ PUBLISHING

travel guides

"NO OTHER CORNER
OF THE EARTH HAS GIVEN RISE,
MORE THAN VENICE,
TO THIS CONSPIRACY
OF ENTHUSIASM"

GUY DE MAUPASSANT
LA VIE ERRANTE (or THE WANDERING LIFE) – 1890

Venice ... La Serenissima, the sinking metropolis, the city of romance par excellence, the victim of rampant tourism ... there's nothing that hasn't already been written about Venice. Whether positive or negative, each of its facets is true. Venice is unique.

Unique because of its lagoon, its inhabitants, and its architecture and artisans, who use centuries-old techniques to recreate masterpieces of glass, silk, velvet, and other materials.

Most importantly, despite the exodus of some of its inhabitants, Venice is alive. It pulsates with students in the Dorsoduro district, merchants in the Rialto, art galleries in San Marco – and with artists, writers, and musicians everywhere.

Above all, Venice has its lagoon; a lagoon where time seems to have stood still; where the fishermen seem straight out of a 17th-century masterpiece; where it's still a pleasure to go rowing in a wooden boat. The calm, green islands of Venice are the lungs the city lacks. Burano, Torcello ... So many magical places to visit, following in the footsteps of Hemingway.

I'm often asked what is the best time of year to discover Venice. I'd say: anytime! Whether it's the shimmering light of summer or the fog in November, every month here offers something special – even in culinary terms.

And the best time of day? Cocktail hour, hands down. That's when Venetians come together at the city's *bacari* to comment on the day's news, often standing, with a Spritz or glass of wine in hand.

This little guide will help you understand a certain Venetian spirit, off the beaten tourist track.

30 unique experiences.

Servane Giol

Servane Giol

Married to a Venetian, Servane has been living in Venice for over twenty years. She opened a theatre school for children and created the Compania Falier theatre group, which develops shows for charity. A mother of four, Servane has also collaborated with *Harper's Bazaar* and *Vogue Germany*.

Thomas Jonglez

The author of *Secret Venice*, which required five years of research and won the award for best travel guide of the year on its release. Thomas lived in Venice for seven years, and still has a small fisherman's house on the northern lagoon – an excellent excuse to return regularly to the most beautiful city in the world.

WHAT YOU WON'T FIND
IN THIS GUIDE

- legends of the Bridge of Sighs
- how to book a gondola tour
- opening hours of the Doge's Palace

WHAT YOU WILL FIND
IN THIS GUIDE

- a bookshop that's taking on water
- some very special crabs
- the best restaurant in Venice
- where to walk on water
- secrets of *baccalà*
- very distinctive ice cream
- medieval artisans

SYMBOLS USED IN
"SOUL OF VENICE"

Less
than €10

€10
to €50

More
than €50

Arrival by boat
is recommended

Make
a reservation

So
Venice!

30 EXPERIENCES

ENTER ST MARK'S
AFTER OPENING HOURS

There's a way to avoid the crowds in St Mark's Basilica, arguably the most beautiful church on the planet: go after public opening hours.

Here's how it's done: about half an hour after the basilica closes to the public, it reopens for Vespers. The meeting point is on the left side of the building. Put away your camera and say or indicate that you intend to pray. The guard posted at the entrance to turn away non-worshippers will let you in.

Once inside, keep a low profile. You're not here as a tourist. Sit down quietly, savour the gorgeous singing and marvel at the basilica in all its splendour.

For true believers, hearing the voices of the choir rise up beneath the golden cupolas is a moment of pure magic.

 BASILICA DI SAN MARCO
PIAZZA SAN MARCO 328
30100 VENEZIA

Vespers time: 5:30 pm (5pm on winter Sundays and holidays), approximately 30 minutes after the closure of the Basilica

HEADING ONTO
THE SILK ROAD

In 1500 there were more than 6,000 looms in operation in the city of Venice. Today, some of the city's wealthy families, such as the Bevilacqua – now in their sixth generation of weavers – continue to keep this tradition alive.

In addition to their exceptional know-how, the Bevilacqua have the added advantage – particularly appreciable to visitors – of owning an amazing wooden loom that dates back to the 18th century and is still in operation. The loom is located behind the showroom and can only be visited by appointment, but the visit offers a truly memorable experience: in a timeless ambiance seven weavers work on velvet, silk, and gold threads using ancestral techniques and patterns that can be found in the historical archives, which include more than 3,500 drawings.

It takes an entire day to make a 30-40 centimetre piece of fabric.

 LUIGI BEVILACQUA
CAMPIELLO DE LA COMARE 1320
30135 VENEZIA

MON–FRI: 9:30am / 1:30pm 2:30pm / 5pm SAT: By appointment SUN: Closed	Visits to the weaving workshop by reservation only +39 041 721 566 luigi-bevilacqua.com	€60 for a group of up to four €15 per person for larger groups

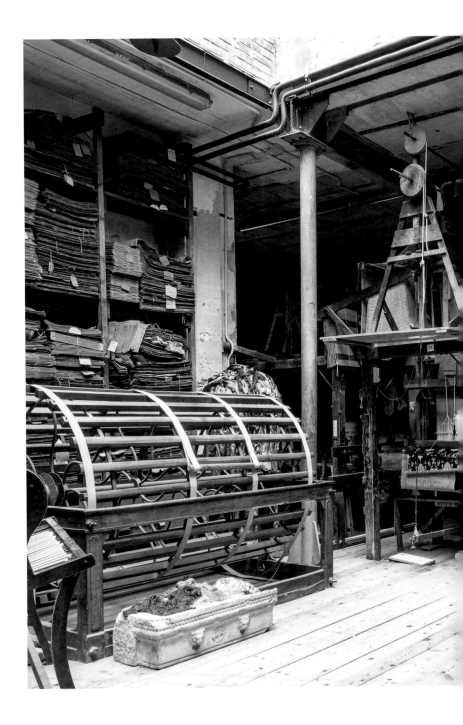

 ## - CATHERINE BUYSE DIAN -

COSTUME DESIGNER

Catherine, you've made dozens of period costume films in Venice. What's the most beautiful era, and where can one find attractive costumes in Venice today?

For me, the most beautiful era is without a doubt the 18th century because it's the most characteristic of Venice in terms of the costumes, masks, Casanova ...

The Palazzo Mocenigo costume museum has some very beautiful original costumes, complete and very well preserved.

For renting a costume, I recommend Stefano Nicolao's workshop; he does many productions for the opera house Teatro La Fenice, as well as for theatre companies.

I use him for my films, whether or not they're in period costume, because his workshop has an endless selection for each era.

Your favourite Venetian fabrics for costumes?

The historical trio Bevilacqua (definitely go see their loom), Rubelli, and Fortuny.

One of your favourite shops for masks?

Definitely Kartaruga in Dorsoduro. This small boutique makes many masks for films. It's interesting to participate in their mask creation workshops (which are held year-round) – small groups in which you can create your own mask.

What's your favourite time of year in Venice?

September, with its film festival at the Lido, which dates back to 1932. It's a magical moment in Venice; it's lovely and warm out, and you can still go for a swim at the beaches of the Lido between films.

As someone who loves to cook, what are your favourite restaurants in Venice?

Antiche Carampane and Al Covo, among others, for their traditional Venetian recipes adapted to modern tastes.

A magical ingredient in Venice?

The little purple artichokes of Sant'Erasmo. Called *castraure*, they're only available in April and May, and they're very rare because each artichoke plant only produces one *castraura* per season. You can find them at the Rialto market when they're in season.

Your favourite hotels?

Oltre il Giardino in San Polo is a charming family-run hotel with a lovely garden, which is rare in Venice for a reasonably priced hotel. Otherwise, I also recommend Palazzo Abadessa to my friends, for the experience of sleeping in a historical palazzo and staying in the 17th-century spirit, since all the furniture and decoration reflect this era.

A mythical film location in Venice?

The church of San Nicolò dei Mendicoli in Santa Marta, which was the setting for Nicolas Roeg's film *Don't Look Now*. Not very well known, it has an exceptional, richly decorated interior with gilded wooden statues.

How do you survive the tourist invasion?

You get out whenever you can. With Venice, you have to escape to make coming back to the city better. In particular, I find refuge in the island of Mazzorbo, thirty minutes by boat from the city centre, near Burano, or in the Dolomites, two hours from Venice. In winter, you can sometimes see the snowy peaks of the Dolomites from the lagoon, on a boat. A magical sight!

# #
03

THE SPECTACULAR
REDENTORE FIREWORKS

Every year since 1577, the Festa del Redentore (Festival of the Redeemer) in Venice takes place on the third Saturday in July. Truly spectacular fireworks mark the occasion, reflecting magically on the surface of Saint Mark's basin. Here are some ways to experience this exceptional event.

> From a boat:

Obviously otherworldly. If you don't have any Venetian friends, you can hire a boat at Brussa: from a small wooden *topetta* (six people) to a majestic *bragozzo* with driver (ten people). From 6pm hundreds of boats begin gathering in Saint Mark's basin after picnicking on the water. The atmosphere is fantastically friendly. Forget trying to leave before the fireworks are over – but who's complaining?

 BRUSSA IS BOAT
FONDAMENTA CANNAREGIO 331
30121 VENEZIA

+39 041 715 787

brussaisboat.it

> From the streets/on foot:

Sitting on the Zattere, or on the banks of the Giudecca Canal, or anywhere along the vast bridge of boats that stretches from the Zattere to the Chiesa del Santissimo Redentore for this one night.

> From Venice's rooftop terraces:

For an ultra-chic and privileged experience, you can rent The Gritti Palace's Redentore Suite and its magnificent 250 square

metre terrace, which offers a spectacular view of the basin and the Basilica of Santa Maria della Salute. Some people in the know who aren't necessarily wealthy rent the suite and split the cost with friends – there's room for 100 on the terrace. A private dinner on the terrace is also an option, before or after the fireworks. Another option is the *altana* on the seventh floor of the Bauer Palazzo hotel, which also has a sublime view. You can make reservations for the dinner the hotel organises on the night of the festival.

- PAOLO LORENZONI -

GENERAL MANAGER AT THE GRITTI PALACE SINCE 2013

Could you give us a short history of the Gritti Palace?

The Gritti Palace is a relatively recent addition to the Venetian hotel landscape. Created in 1948 as an addition to the Grand Hotel (Palazzo Ferro Fini – now the seat of the Veneto Regional Council), the Gritti Palace takes its name from Doge Andrea Gritti, who lived in the palazzo in 1525. It has attracted famous guests such as Ernest Hemingway and Somerset Maugham, who said that "at the Gritti, you are not merely a number ... you are a friend." That's still our philosophy.

Your opinion of Venice?

Venice is unique in the world, not so much for its buildings and the water that surrounds it, but for the people from all around the world who come here: writers, intellectuals, and artists (including recently Damien Hirst) – a good reflection of the city's close ties to art and culture.

An absolute must-see place in Venice?

The Arsenal. To understand the true grandeur of La Serenissima.

Your favourite season?

From November to February, because you can walk around and enjoy the city virtually alone. And I love the foggy days when you can't see anything when you wake up. Then, very gradually, the fog lifts, revealing the monuments and palazzos.

And the rooftop terrace?

When I took over as General Manager, I discovered this abandoned 250-square-metre terrace ... and had the idea of transforming it into a private space for cocktail parties or dinners for up to 100 guests. The view of Venice from up there is unique, and in winter you can even see the snow-covered Dolomites.

Tradition with a modern touch?

When we set about renovating the hotel in 2011, we surveyed over 200 regular customers to find out what they would like to see. Their response was "don't change a thing!" Obviously we added all the modern-day technologies and amenities, but the soul and spirit of the hotel remain intact.

**THE GRITTI PALACE
CAMPO SANTA MARIA DEL GIGLIO
30124 VENEZIA**
+39 041 794 611

TREASURE TROVE
OF A GENIUS

Mariano Fortuny (1871-1949) had many talents: painter, engraver, sculptor, engineer, photographer, inventor, designer, dressmaker, and production designer.

Upon his death, his incredible palace/atelier was gifted to the City of Venice. It has been wonderfully preserved, retaining every ounce of its charm, and is today one of the most beautiful places in Venice, truly worth a visit.

It's all here: his precious library, his collection of paintings, amazing fabrics that entirely cover the walls, miniature theatre scenes, lamps, dress designs, the list goes on ...

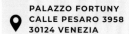

PALAZZO FORTUNY
CALLE PESARO 3958
30124 VENEZIA

WED–MON: 10am / 6pm
during temporary exhibits only
TUE: Closed

+39 041 522 1977

fortuny.visitmuve.it

A FREE
CONCERT

The beautiful Pisani Palace is the second largest palace in Venice after the Doge's Palace; it has been home to the Benedetto Marcello Conservatory since 1912.

The conservatory's 8,000 square metres include a small museum of musical instruments and a spectacular concert hall open to the public, where students perform top quality music free of charge.

 CONSERVATORIO BENEDETTO MARCELLO
SAN MARCO 2810
30124 VENEZIA

+39 041 522 5604   conservatoriovenezia.net

THE BEST
PANORAMIC VIEW
OF VENICE

For the best panoramic view of Venice, forget the overly famous St Mark's Campanile, which is always overloaded with tourists, and head over to the bell tower of San Giorgio Maggiore, on the island of the same name.

Standing 75 metres tall, the tower offers a truly exceptional view: to the north, the Doge's Palace, St Mark's Basilica and the Punto della Dogana, and, even further in the distance, the sublime landscapes of the Southern Lagoon. Another advantage: you'll be practically alone.

Aim to arrive shortly before sunset, after going for a stroll along the Giudecca Canal.

 CAMPANILE DI SAN GIORGIO MAGGIORE
ISOLA SAN GIORGIO MAGGIORE
30124 VENEZIA

May–Sept: MON–SAT: 9:30am / 12:30pm – 2:30pm / 6:30pm
Oct–April: MON–SAT: 9:30am / 12:30pm – 2:30pm / 5pm

MAKE CERAMICS
AMONG ISLAND SHIPYARDS

Venetian by birth, Adele Stefanelli studied and perfected the art of ceramics in Tuscany, China and South Korea. Her ceramics studio on the island of Giudecca lies right next to the Crea shipyard that makes gondolas and wooden boats, giving it a unique atmosphere.

Stefanelli's remarkable creations, with their lagoon-like colours, make fantastic gifts that are far more original than the traditional masks or 'Murano glass' that's actually made in China.

She also organises workshops in her studio by reservation.

 STUDIO DI CERAMICA ADELE STEFANELLI
GIUDECCA 213
CANTIERI CREA - SPAZIO ARTIGIANI

By appointment
+39 347 221 1661
adelestefanelli@gmail.com

adelestefanelli.com

A JOURNEY TO THE END
OF THE WORLD

Located about 45 minutes from Venice by boat, almost at the very end of the southern lagoon, Da Celeste is an exceptional restaurant. The journey from Venice is an unreal and magical experience that will take you past semi-abandoned shipyards and fishermen's houses on stilts, which seem to rise up out of nowhere, delivering you to an extraordinary terrace overlooking the entire southern lagoon.

The restaurant itself upholds the best traditions of Venetian cooking: small shrimp with polenta, shelled spider crab (*granseola*), scallops, exquisite fresh fish . . .

Taking a water taxi to the restaurant from Venice is expensive, so to get there by public transportation, take any vaporetto to the Lido and get off at Santa Maria Elisabetta. From there, take the 11 bus to Pellestrina, get off at the last stop and walk to Da Celeste.

DA CELESTE
VIA VIANELLI 625/B
30126 PELLESTRINA

From March to October:
MON–TUE & THU–SUN: 12noon / 2:30pm – 7pm / 9:15pm

+39 041 967 355

daceleste.it

SLEEP LIKE
YOU'RE ABOARD
A LUXURY LINER

The Palazzo Experimental Hotel opened in 2018 in the delightful Zattere quays. This historic palazzo used to be the headquarters of a maritime shipping company whose name still adorns the facade.

Inside, 32 rooms designed by Dorothée Meilichzon conjure up the maritime spirit, as does the restaurant on the ground floor. Here, everything – from the berth-like banquettes to stripes that are a nod to the gondoliers – evokes the sea and the Lagoon without falling into cliché.

The elegant atmosphere is enhanced by the enormous windows flooded with light, which offer a stunning view of the Giudecca Canal.

 HOTEL IL PALAZZO EXPERIMENTAL
1412 FONDAMENTA ZATTERE AL PONTE LUNGO
30123 VENEZIA

+39 041 098 0200   palazzoexperimental.com

DISCOVER THE ART OF *CICHETI*,
VENETIAN-STYLE TAPAS

Il Bottegon, better known to locals as "Schiavi", is a point of reference in Venice. It is at this wine bar since 1944 that Alessandra and her sons have been cultivating the art of *cicheto* – basically Venetian-style tapas. Small slices of bread are served topped with various ingredients, including tuna and leek, squash and ricotta, and zucchini flowers. These are eaten exclusively standing at the colourful counter, surrounded by Venetian regulars in the cheerful and convivial atmosphere of aperitivo hour. In the warmer months – in other words, often – customers cheerfully spill outside along the canal, where there's a view of one of the last gondola repair workshops.

Note: the *bàcaro* closes at 8:30pm sharp.

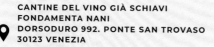

CANTINE DEL VINO GIÀ SCHIAVI
FONDAMENTA NANI
DORSODURO 992. PONTE SAN TROVASO
30123 VENEZIA

MON–SAT: 8:30am / 8:30pm
SUN: Closed

+39 041 523 0034

cantinaschiavi.com

VENICE: BIRTHPLACE OF
THE *SPRITZ* AND THE *BELLINI*

Legend has it that street vendors who sold wine beneath Saint Mark's would keep their wine cool by shifting along with the shadow of its bell tower. That's how, over time, the term ombra (meaning "shadow" or "shade") came to be synonymous with a glass of wine in Venice. But it means so much more than that; it's a declaration of friendship – the daily ritual of heading to one of the city's countless *baccari* for an *ombra*.

Venice is also famous for two cocktails born here and known the world over: the *Bellini* and the *Spritz*.

The *Bellini*, made with Prosecco or champagne and white-peach purée, takes its name from the Venetian painter Giovanni Bellini, and was created in 1948 by Giuseppe Cipriani at Harry's Bar in Venice. Enjoying a *Bellini* at this mythical venue – which remains virtually unchanged from when it first opened – is an absolute must. We prefer savouring one while standing at the bar.

As for the *Spritz*, it's made with Prosecco, Seltzer water and Campari or Aperol, and it varies in colour from red to orange depending on the quantity and quality of the ingredients. This cocktail was born in the first half of the 19th century, when cities in the Veneto region were occupied by Austrian soldiers. They would ask waiters to dilute the local wine with water to make it lighter. *Spritzen* ("to spray") gave rise to the name *Spritz*.

ICE CREAM
WITH A VIEW

You would think that the Gelateria Todaro is nothing more than a tourist trap, given its location between St. Mark's Square and the lagoon. But with its beautiful terrace overlooking the San Marco Basin, this ice cream parlour, founded in 1948, remains one of the best places in Venice to enjoy this dairy treat. And what is the best flavour? Undoubtedly the pistachio with real nut pieces. The pistachios come from Bronte on the slopes of Mount Etna in Sicily, and are considered by many to be the best variety in the world. It's also worth stopping at the bar to admire the Murano glass ceiling made by Barovier in 1979.

For many Venetians, the sunny waterfront of Zattere in the Dorsoduro district is the best place for a stroll. This is where, since 1920, the Gelateria Nico has made by hand its famous Gianduiotto: an ice cream made from gianduja (chocolate and nuts) covered with whipped cream. It's the perfect place to stop, relax, and admire the island of Giudecca.

 GELATERIA AL TODARO
SAN MARCO 3
30124 VENEZIA

MON–SUN: 8:30am / 6:00pm
+39 041 528 5165
al-todaro.it

GELATERIA NICO
FONDAMENTA ZATTERE
 AL PONTE LONGO 922
30123 VENEZIA

FRI–WED: 6:30am / 9:00pm
THU: Closed
+39 041 522 5293
gelaterianico.com

RENT THE *PIANO NOBILE* OF VENICE'S MOST BEAUTIFUL PALAZZOS

Owned by the Singer Polignac family since the 19th century, the magnificent Palazzo Contarini Polignac is one of most beautiful in Venice, its Renaissance façade reflected in the Grand Canal. And here's an insider secret: the family lets one of the two sublime "noble floors" (five rooms), allowing guests to immerse themselves in the splendour of this family of patrons, painters, and musicians.

It is a genuine privilege to spend a few days in these rooms. You can play the piano that once belonged to the patron of music Winnaretta Singer, Princesse Edmond de Polignac (1865-1943), and sleep in magnificent canopy beds from the Palazzio Labia and from the collection of Charles de Besteigui.

**PALAZZO POLIGNAC
DORSODURO 874
30123 VENEZIA**

palazzocontarinipolignac.com

THE MOST BEAUTIFUL
GLASSWARE IN VENICE

Navigating the countless shops in Venice that sell glass (of occasionally dubious taste) isn't always easy. So, to avoid buying glass made in China, head to these reliable sources:

> L'Angolo del Passato ("Nook from the Past") is one of the best places for high-quality Murano glass. Giordana Naccari is the heart and soul of this small boutique. Born and raised in Murano, she has developed her own line of glass alongside her collection of old glass, which includes unique pieces by major names such as Venini, Cenedese, and Saviati. Giordana also offers the latest collections by Marcantonio Brandolini (Laguna B) and Giberto Arrivabene (Giberto Venezia).

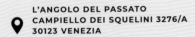

L'ANGOLO DEL PASSATO
CAMPIELLO DEI SQUELINI 3276/A
30123 VENEZIA

MON: 3:30pm / 7:30pm	
TUE-SAT: 9:30am / 12:30pm	+39 041 528 7896
SUN: Closed	

> At Massimo Micheluzzi (one of the greatest contemporary glass artists in Venice), his two daughters Elena and Margherita recently created a "mini Micheluzzi" line, as well as a line of "soft" glasses, each of which is unique and seems to melt in your hands.

 MASSIMO MICHELUZZI
PONTE DELLE MERAVEGIE 1071
30123 VENEZIA

MON-SAT: 10am / 7pm
SUN: Closed

+39 041 528 2190

massimomicheluzzi.it

> Since 1921, the Venini household has been renowned not only for the technical quality of its creations, but also, and more importantly, for the fact that is has always worked with the best artists, designers and architects of its times. Not to put too fine a point on it, but these days, if you have money and want a beautiful object in Murano glass, head to Venini.

All the greatest Italian names of the 20th century have brought their personal touch to Venini: Carlo Scarpa and Tommaso Buzzi from the outset; Franco Albini and Fulvio Bianconi in the 1950s; and during the 1990s, the house became more international, associating with famous names in architecture, such as Matteo Thun, Tadao Ando and Ron Arad.

The store is perfectly located on the Piazzetta dei Leoncini, just a stone's throw from St. Mark's Basilica. You'll find all the new collaborations, as well as a few reissued artistic pieces.

VENINI
SAN MARCO 314
30124 VENEZIA

MON–SAT: 10:00am / 7:00pm
SUN: 10:30am / 6:30pm

+39 041 522 4045

venini.com

> Venice-born Alessandro Zoppi has spent his life collecting Murano glasses. The glasses date from 1700 to the 1940s, and most are signed by some of the most important master glassmakers of Venice, including Zecchin, Martinuzzi, and Scarpa. Zoppi's gallery is home to 300 years of glass history. Some pieces are organised by colour rather than chronological order.

If you are lucky, you may be granted the honour of being invited into his palace on the Grand Canal; it is among the very few palaces in Venice with Tiepolo frescos on the ceiling. Zoppi's wife Alessandra summarised it in these terms: "At home there is *tutto* – in other words, the entire collection. It is such a big collection that neither one of us can say with exact certainty how many artefacts there are in the collection."

 GALLERIA ALESSANDRO ZOPPI
2671 CAMPO SAN MAURIZIO
30124 VENEZIA

| MON–SAT: 10:30am / 12:30pm – 3:30pm / 7pm | +39 041 528 7579 | zoppiantiques.it |

PHOTO CREDIT: MICHAEL JAMES O'BRIEN

- GIBERTO ARRIVABENE -

FOUNDER AND CREATOR OF GIBERTO VENEZIA
VENETIAN BY BIRTH

**When and how did
you begin designing
glassware?**

My family is Venetian going back to the 14th century, and we own some very beautiful sets of antique glassware. Whenever a glass would break,

I'd go to Murano to have it remade. I gradually began to design them myself. First for myself, then as wedding or birthday presents. A collection was born that now includes vases, frames, sculptures, and more.

What's the situation like for glassmakers in Venice right now?

It's a complicated period. The *fornace* are floundering because production costs have gone up and there are fewer and fewer master glassmakers. Not to mention imitations, which it's difficult to protect yourself against because there isn't any form of patenting in Murano. Plus, it isn't easy to distinguish genuine glass items from fakes.

An absolute must-see place in Venice?

The Basilica dei Frari is my favourite church. But also the Basilica dei Santi Giovanni e Paolo because that's where the tomb of Marcantonio Bragadin is located, which I love.

Your favourite restaurants?

Harry's Bar, Trattoria alla Madonna, and the restaurant in the Aman Venice.

Speaking of the Aman, the hotel is located in your family's palazzo ...

Yes, since 2014. My family has always lived in the palazzo;

what used to be my mother's room is now the famous Tiepolo suite. And we still live there, on the top floor, with my wife (Vice President of Christie's Italy) and our five children. It's an incredible luxury to have a hotel like the Aman right downstairs from us.

"When you grow up in Venice, it becomes increasingly difficult to leave the city with every passing year."

Do your children want to stay in Venice?

Yes. The two oldest have created their own brand of *friulane* (Venetian slippers) called ViBi Venezia. I think that when you grow up in Venice, it becomes increasingly difficult to leave the city with every passing year. It has such a unique quality of life, such a particular rhythm, that it seems hard to adapt to other cities.

Venice is an affordable, international city with divinely good food, in addition to all its beauty. And my friends are here.

SLEEP IN THE WORLD'S ONLY BEDROOM
WITH A TIEPOLO FRESCO

In 2014 the Arrivabene family's enormous 16th-century Palazzo Papadopoli on the Grand Canal (near the Rialto) was opened as the exquisite Aman Venice hotel.

Amongst its 24 rooms, the Alcova Tiepolo Suite (measuring 103 m^2) is perhaps the only hotel room in the world where you can sleep beneath a magnificent fresco by the famous Venetian painter, Giovanni Battista Tiepolo.

In fact, the painter himself lived in this palazzo in the 18th century, and his theatrical frescoes are a superb example of the Rococo style.

L'ALCOVA TIEPOLO SUITE - HOTEL AMAN VENICE
PALAZZO PAPADOPOLI
CALLE TIEPOLO 1364
30125 VENEZIA

+39 041 270 7333   aman.com

Frittelle

 TONOLO
CALLE S. PANTALON, 3764
30123 VENEZIA

TUE-SAT: 7:45am / 8pm
SUN: 7:45am / 1pm   +39 041 523 7209   pasticceria-tonolo-venezia.business.site
MON: Closed

FRITTERS TO GO
CRAZY FOR

Venice is one of the rare cities where the pastries still follow the seasons and the rhythm of the religious calendar. As a result, you'll find *frittelle* (*fritole* in Venetian) for only a few weeks in February, around the time of Carnival. Invented around 1700, these delicious fritters (with raisins and, more often than not, pine nuts) come in various iterations: "plain" (our favourite), as well as with cream, orange peel, zabaione, etc. The quality depends on where you buy them; Rosa Salva, Tonolo, and Dal Nono Colussi are three sure bets. But be warned, the rareness of the product and the exceptional taste can lead to serious addiction!

On 1 November the beans of the dead (*fave dei morti*) appear – small, almond-flavoured, and quite crunchy tricolour balls (pink, brown and cream), whose shape is reminiscent of the legumes they are named after. A few days later, on the day of the eponymous festival (11 November), you'll find the *San Martino* – a large shortbread in the shape of a horse-riding Saint Martin (who gave half his coat to a poor man), covered with icing, candies, small chocolates and other sweets. Children are crazy about them and often beg for them by beating on pots and pans like others do for treats on Halloween.

ROSA SALVA CAMPO SANTI GIOVANNI E PAOLO, 6779 30122 VENEZIA	DAL NONO COLUSSI CALLE LUNGA DE SAN BARNABA, 2867/A 30123 VENEZIA
MON–SUN: 8am / 8pm — +39 041 522 7949 — rosasalva.it	WED–SUN: 9am / 1pm – 3:30pm / 5pm — MON–TUE: Closed — +39 041 523 1871 — dalnonocolussi.com

THE BEST SANDWICH
IN VENICE

At first glance, Ai Nomboli isn't very likely to make you want to stop there. It's a bar more or less like any other on a busy street near Campo San Polo, with a small terrace that's of no particular interest. But if you're pressed for time or tired of paying a fortune for a bland lunch, Ai Nomboli offers what are quite simply the best sandwiches in town.

The choice and quality of ingredients is spectacular, and for some it might even be the best *panini* they've ever eaten.

AI NOMBOLI
RIO TERÀ DEI NOMBOLI 2717/C
30125 VENEZIA

MON-FRI: 7am / 9pm
SAT: 7am / 3pm   +39 041 523 0995
SUN: Closed

A TRATTORIA
TO LOSE YOURSELF IN

You don't simply happen upon Antiche Carampane, a trattoria hidden away in the labyrinth of narrow alleyways of the San Polo district.

Despite its name – 'old whores', a vestige from the Serenissima era, when this was the district of ill repute – Antiche Carampane is actually one of the best restaurants in Venice.

There is a pleasant, family atmosphere and the cuisine is top quality, specialising in fish and seafood. In summer, don't miss the *crudo di pesce*, an assortment of raw fish, or the pasta with *bottarga* (salted, cured fish roe).

 ANTICHE CARAMPANE
RIO TERÀ DE LE CARAMPANE 1911
30125 VENEZIA

TUE–SAT: for lunch and dinner
SUN & MON: Closed

+39 041 524 0165

antichecarampane.com

- FRANCESCO AGOPYAN -

TRATTORIA ANTICHE CARAMPANE

Francesco, when was your restaurant established?

Antiche Carampane was created in 1983; my mother's brothers (Nani and Guido) bought this old *trattoria*, which at the time was located in a half-hidden neighbourhood in Venice where hardly anyone went, except for students. Initially the restaurant was only open during the day for the construction workers in the neighbourhood. Then, very gradually, it began to stay open at night for the Venetians.

From the start, my uncle Nani, a fine connoisseur of cooking and the history of Venice (he was the son of a Rialto merchant), offered a rather innovative cuisine. He was the first to serve raw fish, and fish and clams seasoned with Parmesan, and to update old recipes like *spaghetti in cassopipa* (which is still just as popular 35 years later) – in short, somewhat idiosyncratic dishes. After a few years, my mother joined him and, beginning in 2004, so did I.

Where do you buy your fish?

The restaurant has always had very close ties to the Rialto market – in part because of its proximity, in part because my grandfather had a fish stand there. Ever since I was very little, I've been hearing about fish and about the market as a strategic spot in the city. My grandfather always said: "When the Rialto market closes, Venice will be a ghost town."
I got into the habit of going there every morning to choose my fish and vegetables from three or four stalls, with whose vendors I've developed friendships and mutual esteem over the years. Our restaurant is naturally closed on Sunday and Monday, when the market itself is closed, since the fishermen don't work on those days. To this day, we offer local cuisine using seasonal products that the lagoon provides – from both land and sea.

Can you explain the Armenian origins of your surname?

Our family (Agopyan is my surname) has Armenian roots; during the genocide in Turkey in 1915, my grandfather was able to leave Istanbul via Izmir and take refuge in Venice thanks to the Mekhitarist monks. He entered the Armenian Moorat-Raphael College, where he studied before becoming an entrepreneur. For as long as it has existed, Venice has had contact with the Armenian people, and the city's Armenian community has grown over the centuries. In 1715 Father Mekhitar settled on the Island of San Lazzaro, founding the so-called "Island of the Armenians". As for me, over the years I've discovered a strong connection to the Armenian people and wonderful nation of Armenia, which culminated in a trip I made there in April 2019.

"When the Rialto market closes, Venice will be a ghost town."

THE ART OF VENETIAN
VELVET SLIPPER SHOES

Invented around 1800, *furlane* (or *friulane*) are slipper-shoes created from recycled materials, with soles made out of old fabric and bicycle tyres. Gondoliers began to wear them after the First World War as the rubber soles didn't scratch their gondolas, were supple and didn't slip.

The Piedàterre shop in the Rialto offers a colourful and diverse range of these slippers while respecting the tradition of velvet and linen uppers.

Perfect for wearing at home – and, in some cases, even for strolling down the street.

PIEDÀTERRE
RUGA DEGLI ORESI 60
30125 VENEZIA

DAILY: 10am / 7pm

piedaterre-venice.com

SHOP AT THE WORLD'S
MOST BEAUTIFUL MARKET

If you're Venetian, you already know; but if you've only rented an apartment or palazzo for a few days, you absolutely must – yes, *must* – shop at the sublime Rialto market at least once.

Firstly, it's clearly the most beautiful market in the world: buying fish, fruits, or vegetables (all of excellent quality) here along the Grand Canal, right near the Rialto, is truly a rare pleasure. As is enjoying a glass of white wine or a Spritz at one of the nearby bars (like the lovely Naranzaria) after you're done shopping.

Secondly, the market is under threat from the pressures of real estate and tourism. In the words of the grandfather of Francesco Agopyan, of the Antiche Carampane restaurant: "When the Rialto market closes, Venice will be a ghost town."

 CAMPIELLO DE LA PESCARIA
30122 VENEZIA

TUE–SAT: 7:30am / 12noon
SUN–MON: Closed

THE WONDER ROOM
OF THE GREAT
VENETIAN EXPLORERS

The remarkable Museum of Natural History of Venice houses a magnificent wonder room that offers a motley mix of precious, rare, bizarre and even grotesque objects. There is an albino Bambi enthroned in the middle of shells and butterflies or a strange two-headed animal near a monstrous crab.

In the neighboring rooms, you can also admire the extraordinary collections of animals of three Venetian explorers: Giovanni Miani and Giuseppe Reali and also, more recently, Giancarlo Ligabue, who gives his name to the museum.

Children just love it.

MUSEO DI STORIA NATURALE DI VENEZIA GIANCARLO LIGABUE
SALIZADA DEL FONTEGO DEI TURCHI 1730
30135 VENEZIA

TUE–FRI: 9am / 5pm
SAT–SUN: 10:30am / 5pm
MON: Closed

+39 041 270 0303

msn.visitmuve.it

THE TEMPLE
OF *BACCALÀ*

In 1432 the great Venetian sailor Pietro Querini was shipwrecked near the island of Sandøy in Norway. There, he discovered dried cod. He brought it back to Venice and it became a culinary specialty. Six centuries later, every local restaurant has its own family recipe and secrets for preparing the dish.

Nonno Ettore, the grandfather of the current owners of "Baccalà Veneto" (*baccalà* means cod in Italian), which has just one table and four stools, is the man behind the best recipes. In this little shop, cod is prepared in 60 different ways, all of which can either be ordered to go or eaten on site. Varieties include *Mantecato, Umido, alla Vicentina*, garlic-free, gluten-free, or lactose-free.

Edoardo and Paolo also prepare *panini* that they will happily fill with the *baccalà* of your choice, eg. with Trevisano radicchio, or with tomato, which is Edoardo's personal favourite.

If that weren't enough, there are beautiful little tins of cod decorated with the names of the districts of Venice available for sale; ideal souvenirs and perfectly suited to travelling.

 BACCALÀ VENETO
SESTIERE SAN POLO 414
30125 VENEZIA

DAILY: 9:30am / 8pm in summer –
10:30am / 7pm in winter

+39 041 476 3571

baccalaveneto.com

A BOOKSHOP THAT'S
TAKING ON WATER!

The Acqua Alta bookshop, hidden behind San Marco and regularly flooded, displays its stock in rather unusual ways ... Here, bathtubs, canoes and even a gondola have been transformed into shelving for old and new books.

Despite the apparent disarray, Luigi Frizzo, the owner, knows exactly where to find each book and will guide you enthusiastically through his labyrinth in search of treasures such as *The Little Prince* in Venetian dialect.

For photographers in search of stunning panoramas, climbing the book staircase is an absolute must for a magnificent view of the Venetian Lagoon.

LIBRERIA ACQUA ALTA
CALLE LUNGA SANTA MARIA FORMOSA 5176B
30122 VENEZIA

| DAILY: 9:15am / 7:45pm | +39 041 296 0841 | libreriaacquaaltavenezia.myadj.it |

WHERE THE ANGEL
PASSES BY

The exceptional Tribuna within the magnificent Palazzo Grimani near Santa Maria Formosa was the original home of the collection of Greek and Roman sculptures owned by the Grimani family. However, upon the death of patriarch Giovanni Grimani in 1587, the works of art were given as gifts to the Republic of Venice. They were initially moved to safety in the Biblioteca Marciana, before being transferred to the Doge's Palace.

The collection, displaced for more than four centuries, eventually returned to its original home thanks to the non-profit organisation "Venetian Heritage". The result is breathtaking.

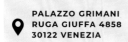 **PALAZZO GRIMANI**
RUGA GIUFFA 4858
30122 VENEZIA

TUE-SUN: 10am / 7pm MON: Closed	+39 041 241 1507	polomusealeveneto.beniculturali.it/musei/ museo-di-palazzo-grimani

WALKING
ON WATER

The Celestia vaporetto stop, at the north of the city, marks the start of one of the most original and poetic walks in Venice. On a metal footbridge attached to the exterior walls of the Arsenal, you can walk to the Bacini vaporetto stop in 5 to 10 minutes, as if you were suspended above the water.

From this place far, very far, off the beaten track and hordes of tourists, the view of the cemetery island of San Michele as well as of Murano is magnificent.

At the end of the walk, two options: take the footbridge in the opposite direction or continue on your way, this time by taking the vaporetto as the area at the end of the island is a military zone closed to the public.

 SUSPENDED WALK ON THE NORTH WALLS OF THE ARSENAL

Vaporettos Celestia and Bacini

LEAVE YOUR BALLET SLIPPERS
ON DIAGHILEV'S GRAVE

Across the water from Fondamente Nove, the island of San Michele is home to one of the most beautiful cemeteries in the world – an oasis of peace that is the final resting place of Igor Stravinsky, Emilio Vedova and Ezra Pound, among others.

The cemetery's Orthodox section is the setting for a lovely tradition: every year, dancers from around the world visit the tomb of Sergei Diaghilev, director of the Ballets Russes, to leave their ballet shoes in a final tribute to him.

 ISOLA DI SAN MICHELE
30141 VENEZIA

DAILY: 8:15am / 4pm	+39 041 729 2811	

AN APERITIF
IN THE COUNTRYSIDE

The rich soil on the island of Sant'Erasmo has always provided Venice with a variety of vegetables, including the famous purple artichokes. It was here in the early 2000s, on the banks of a canal with a superb view over the entire northern lagoon, that Michel Thoulouze established his vineyard, which produces Orto di Venezia: a top quality white wine, and the only wine cultivated within the territory of the city of Venice.

This marvellous spot welcomes small groups and offers tastings by reservation – a truly exceptional experience.

 **ORTO DI VENEZIA**
VIA DELLE MOTTE 1
30141 VENEZIA

Tour and tasting (reservations on the website): THU–TUE: 10am / 12:30pm – 2:30pm / 6pm WED: Closed	ortodivenezia.com	€15 per person (minimum 10 people) Vaporetto stop: Capannone

GO ON A MAGICAL SPIRITUAL RETREAT ON
AN ISLAND IN THE LAGOON

The island of San Francesco del Deserto is an exceptional place, possibly one of the most beautiful in the entire Venetian Lagoon. To get a real idea of the island and the life of its monks, we recommend doing a retreat there for a few days.

After making your reservation by phone (in Italian only), you'll be welcomed to Burano by a monk who will come to pick you up by boat: there is no public transport to the island.

The retreat, whose days are rhythmically structured by the seven canonical hours, offers a true immersion in monastic life. Between the services, you'll still be free to do whatever you like with your time. The island being as beautiful as it is, most retreat participants go for walks and meditate in the exceptional garden, an enchanting place where long rows of cypress trees form shaded paths.

St Francis of Assisi is said to have stayed on the island in 1220 or 1224.

 ISLAND OF SAN FRANCESCO DEL DESERTO
30142 BURANO
VENEZIA

Retreats are possible
from Friday to Sunday
or from Tuesday to Thursday

Reservations for spiritual
retreats (in Italian):
+39 041 528 6863
sfdeserto@libero.it

sanfrancescodeldeserto.it

SOME IMPORTANT PRACTICAL ADVICE

Avoid the period between June and September: besides the heat, the mosquitoes are almost unbearable!

The Franciscan Rule, unlike that followed in Benedictine monasteries for example, does not impose silence. Talking is allowed at meals, with the monks, in the gardens, and so on. So if silence is what you're after, we strongly recommend coming either in winter (when fog over the Lagoon adds to the mysterious and magical atmosphere) or during the week. Women are welcome, as are couples, though you will have to stay in separate rooms. Every day of the retreat features a commentary, in Italian, on a passage from the Bible – or a personal meeting with a monk, depending on the number of guests at the time.

- JANE DA MOSTO -

PRESIDENT AND CO-FOUNDER OF "WE ARE HERE VENICE"
NON-PROFIT ASSOCIATION FOR THE PROTECTION OF VENICE AND ITS LAGOON

Jane, you've been living in Venice for over 20 years; have you seen the lagoon change?

Yes. The lagoon is very fragile. It was fragile 20 years ago and is even more so today, after two decades without policies to protect it and the failure to implement the first Special Law of 1973 (created after the tremendous *acqua alta* of 1966), which recommended doing everything to stem the erosion of the lagoon. Nothing was done to stop this erosion, which is the real problem, caused by the passage of cruise ships and the excavation of large navigation channels to allow them to pass.

The *barene** alone can't retain all the sediment that the boats and wind stir up. While the effect of the passage of small boats is offset by the natural processes of the *barena*, that's not the case for those of large cruise ships, which displace large volumes of water each time they pass, weakening the city's foundations.

Finally, these cruise ships heavily pollute the surrounding air, and there is a real risk of accident; in 2019 there were some very close calls involving ships almost hitting the city's quays on several occasions.

Is the Venetian lagoon unique?

Humans have been living on the Venetian lagoon for over 1,000 years, so they've gradually shaped it according to their needs. About 500 years ago, the accumulation of river sediment was causing the lagoon to disappear. A man named Cristoforo Sabbadino saved the lagoon by redirecting the course of the rivers to the north and south.

What's the problem with *acqua alta*?

There has always been *acqua alta* – a result of the combined effects of the tides and wind in particular. However, its impact has increased recently due to global warming and rising sea levels.

Individually, what can tourists do to help Venice?

Stay for more than one night and avoid Airbnb, which operates without virtually any human contact. It also decreases the number of apartments available to residents, and is contributing to the rise in property prices that is driving residents away.

Your favourite place in Venice?

There are so many, but I love to walk in northern Venice from Calle de la Celestia to Bacini. The route takes you along the northern walls of the Arsenal, from where you can see the open lagoon with San Michele and Murano to the left. There's a small garden at the end of the walkway where you can rest.

Another walk: on Lazzaretto Nuovo (a former quarantine island) and Sant' Erasmo to enjoy the sunset amidst artichoke plantations.

Your favourite restaurant?

My advice is to go shopping at the Rialto market and to take the time to talk to the people behind the stalls; the vegetable growers have a story for each fruit and vegetable they sell. And then there's also the extraordinary variety of fish available at the fish market.

A souvenir to bring back home?

A pillow called "Laguna" designed by my friend Stella Cattana, available at her shop near San Samuele (Salizada San Samuele). It was inspired by our days together on the lagoon, and a portion of the profits from its sale goes to our association.

How do you survive the tourist invasion?

By hopping on a boat and heading to islands like Mazzorbo and Pellestrina where tourists don't go.

Barena: A term specific to the Venetian lagoons, the *barena* is marshy terrain periodically submerged by the tides that promotes exchanges between the sea, river, and lagoon. It moderates the effects of the waves caused by navigation. The association "We Are Here Venice" has created a map of the *barene* to show where they can be seen.

#28

RENT A PRIVATE ISLAND
IN THE NORTHERN LAGOON

For those who would rather avoid the crowds when visiting Venice and its lagoon, the island of Santa Cristina – half an hour by boat from the centre of Venice, near Burano and Torcello – is a luxurious private island that you can rent for several days.

From its organic vegetable gardens and vines to its ecological fish farm and family of peacocks strolling nonchalantly around the gardens, everything here will fill you with peace and tranquillity.

The pretty villa has nine rooms and can accommodate up to sixteen people. Yoga courses can also be arranged, and you can hire a boat with a skipper.

📍 **ISOLA PRIVATA SANTA CRISTINA**

+43 664 822 5080
info@veniceprivateisland.

veniceprivateisland.com

HAVE LUNCH IN
THE GARDEN
OF PARADISE

Ernest Hemingway wrote his novel Across the *River and into the Trees* at the very charming Locanda Cipriani, where he lived for several months. You'll sleep like a baby in these simple rooms, which exude perfect old-fashioned charm.

The magnificent bucolic garden and shady arbour are also wonderful spots for Sunday lunch; you'll feel like you're in the countryside. Prolong the pleasure with grappa, limoncello and coffee, before visiting the exceptional neighbouring cathedral of Santa Maria Assunta, founded in 639AD.

LOCANDA CIPRIANI
PIAZZA SANTA FOSCA 29
30142 TORCELLO

WED–MON: 12noon / 3pm – 7pm / 9pm
TUE: Closed
Closed in January

+39 041 730 150

locandacipriani.com

DISCOVER
SOFT-SHELL CRAB

Moeca is one of the great culinary specialties of Venice. Twice a year (from the end of January to May and from the end of September to the end of November), the fishermen of the Venetian Lagoon (Burano and Chioggia) head out to fish for crab at a very specific moment in the crustaceans' life cycle – when the crabs have just molted their old exoskeleton and their new shell is at its softest.

Once caught, the crabs spend an entire night in a preparation of beaten eggs. They are then fried and eaten whole, in one bite, shell included. It's a must!

The crab's shell starts to harden about four days after it has molted. To eat the crabs fresh (and not frozen), it is best to eat them within the three days that follow the moment the crabs molt their old shells, so finding a trustworthy restaurant is essential. These restaurants include Da Romano (Burano), Lele (Murano – lunchtime only) and in Venice at the Trattoria alla Madonna near the Rialto Market.

TRATTORIA DA ROMANO VIA SAN MARTINO DX 221 30012 BURANO	TRATTORIA BUSA ALLA TORRE "DA LELE" CAMPO SANTO STEFANO 3 30141 MURANO	ALLA MADONNA CALLE DELLA MADONNA 569 30125 VENEZIA
MON: 12noon / 3pm – 6:30pm / 8:30pm WED–SAT: 12noon / 3pm – 6:30pm / 8:30pm SUN: 12noon / 3pm TUE: Closed +39 041 730 030 / daromano.it	DAILY: 11:30am / 3:30pm +39 041 739 662	THU–TUE: 12noon / 3pm 6:45pm / 10:15pm WED: Closed +39 041 522 3824 ristorantealllamadonna.com

**We never reveal the 31ˢᵗ address
in the "Soul of" series because it's strictly confidential.
Up to you to find it!**

A GALLERY WORTH
LOSING YOURSELF IN

Walking on sand in the middle of Venice; under the ruins of the old Sant'Apollinare opera house; there are no signs or advertising boards indicating where to find this infinitely charming art gallery whose water gate opens onto an exquisite canal.

This is where art historian Beatrice Burati exhibits a select group of artists, such as Tristano di Robilant and Andrew Huston, who have an intrinsic link with the city of Venice.

Here is a clue to discovering this well-kept secret: not too far from Campo San Polo, near the entrance to a very luxurious hotel that opened a few years ago in one of the most beautiful private palaces in Venice, you will find a Venetian door that opens onto a wooded courtyard …

MANY THANKS TO

GIOVANNI GIOL, my husband, who was the first to introduce me to the Venice of the Venetians over 20 years ago.

AMBRA, LEONARDO, AMERIGO and GREGORIO, my children, for having approved and tested all the *cicheti* and *tramezzini* in the guide.

FRANCESCA LANARO, GABI WAGNER and ALESSANDRO BELJOIOSO for their magnificent photos without which this book would not have been possible.

CATHERINE BUYSE DIAN, JANE DA MOSTO, GIBERTO ARRIVABENE and PAOLO LORENZONI, my friends, for their time and for giving me each an original point of view on their city.

ARRIGO CIPRIANI, FRANCESCO AGOPYAN and LELE for their participation in the preservation of Venetian culinary traditions.

GIORDANA NACCARI, ALESSANDRA and ALESSANDRO ZOPPI for revealing me the art of glass through the centuries.

KAROLE VAIL, ANDREW HUSTON and BEATRICE ANDERSON for continuing to create an artistic pulse in Venice.

FANY PÉCHIODAT for her ideas, her point of view and her enthusiasm.

Congratulations above all to all the Venetians who courageously fight regularly against the acqua alta and the tourist affluence and allow Venice to be as beautiful as ever.

And thank you Venice!

This book was created by:
Servane Giol, co-author
Thomas Jonglez, co-author
Francesca Lanaro, photographer
Clara Mari, illustrator
Emmanuelle Willard Toulemonde, layout
Sophie Schlondorff, translation
Matt Gay and Jana Gough, editing
Laura Perreca, proofreading
Thomas Jonglez, publishing

You can write to us at contact@soul-of-cities.com
Follow us on Instagram on @soul_of_guides

THANK YOU

© JONGLEZ 2020
Registration of copyright: October 2020 - Edition: 01
ISBN: 978-2-36195-331-7
Printed in Slovakia by Polygraf